THE FIVE-MINUTE GUIDE TO FRCP 30(B)(6) DEPOSITIONS

JIM GARRITY, ESQ.

THE FIVE-MINUTE GUIDE TO FRCP 30(B)(6) DEPOSITIONS

Ross and Rubin Publishers, LLC

New York, New York

The Five-Minute Guide to FRCP 30(b)(6) Depositions

Copyright © 2019 by Jim Garrity

All rights reserved.

No part of this book may be reproduced in any form or by any electronic or mechanical means, including information storage and retrieval systems, without written permission from the author, except for the use of brief quotations in a book review.

While all attempts have been made to verify the information provided in this publication, neither the author nor the publisher assumes any responsibility for errors, omissions or contrary interpretations of the subject matter herein.

The views expressed are the personal views and opinions of the author. The reader is responsible for his or her own actions.

Adherence to all applicable laws and regulations, including international, federal, state and local governing professional licensing, business practices, advertising and all other aspects of doing business in the United States, Canada, or any other jurisdiction relating to the practice of law is the sole responsibility of the purchaser or reader. The reader should be governed by the rules and regulations pertinent to the jurisdictions in which they practice. Neither the author nor the publisher assumes any responsibility or liability whatsoever on the behalf of the purchaser or reader of these materials. Any perceived slight of any individual, organization or culture is purely unintentional.

The designated representative deposition, promulgated in 1970 as FRCP 30(b)(6) by the U.S. Supreme Court, may be the single-most valuable, and overlooked, weapon in the sophisticated litigator's arsenal. It should be used in *every* case where one or more parties are organization.

— ADAM GEFFEN, LITIGATION CONSULTANT

FOREWORD

Hope is not a good plan. Pertinent here is that you can't win cases by hoping deponents will know what you think they know.

This is where Federal Rule of Civil Procedure 30(b)(6) comes in. The rule allows you to designate specific topics and compel an entity to prepare a witness to testify on those topics.

The result is that, with proper crafting of the Rule 30(b)(6) topic list (which this guide shows how to do), you can obligate the organization to prepare and produce a witness or witnesses to testify about most key issues. Such testimony binds the *entity itself*, just as individual witnesses are bound by their own testimony.

Of equal benefit is the fact that questions posed to the designated representatives are not limited to the topics in the notice. In other words, and as Jim Garrity points out, the topic notice is a starting point, not an exclusive list.

Rule 30(b)(6) depositions minimize or eliminate finger-pointing among deponents as to who knows what. Prior to the rule's adoption, litigators had to guess at which witnesses knew what. And even if they guessed correctly, they often found that once depositions were under way, corporate witnesses would play "testimonial hot potato," claiming that it wasn't them, but someone else, who knew the answers.

Thus, prior to the rule's adoption, litigators wasted extraordinary time and money nailing down even basic or obvious facts.

Rule 30(b)(6) was adopted to address these twin evils. In depositions under this rule, the designated deponent(s) *must* provide responsive information, failing which the organization will suffer the consequences.

And those consequences, in the form of monetary sanctions or orders *in limine* barring the organization from repairing the testimony later, are severe. Sanctions can be imposed for a designated representative's failure to speak on listed topics even if the information sought is not known by any current employee of the organization. In such situations, many courts have held, the organization had an obligation to pore through its records to find the answer, or even reach out to former employees as part of its due diligence preparation efforts.

This book, which is excerpted and revised from Jim Garrity's practice masterwork on on the art and science of depositions, *10,000 Depositions Later: The Premier Litigation Guide for Superior Deposition Practice* (available on Amazon), is a timely, thoroughly-researched expert-level guide. It covers every conceivable issue and nuance in a short, enjoyable read. Make good use of it and good luck.

Charles R. Jones
  Expert Analyst, Federal Rules of Procedure
  Washington, DC

PREFACE

Thank you for choosing this guide.

I decided to begin creating a series of advanced guides on deposition skills and techniques after reading studies showing that the civil trial in our judicial system is on the verge of complete extinction.

One legal scholar, Professor Marc Galanter, found that about only about one percent of all federal lawsuits now end in a trial. State court lawsuits have similarly fallen off the cliff. One article in a business publication, citing Professor Galanter's studies, was titled "Will There Be A Next Generation of Trial Lawyers?", underscoring the disappearance of the American court trial.

Without question, depositions are the new trials. That's because depositions are for most lawyers the only place any witness will ever testify. This means that in most lawsuits, the outcome is decided by deposition testimony.

There are many books for sale about deposition strategies and tactics. So, what hasn't been written already? The answer is, everything.

The books, treatises, and seminars for sale overwhelmingly address the mechanical aspects of depositions. They tell us to organize documents, to mark exhibits as we use them, and to work from an outline to make sure we don't miss anything. These "tips" are, for the most part, instinctive and need not be taught for an exorbitant price. Indeed, most lawyers learned them in a law school trial practice course.

I began to wonder about the backgrounds of those offering up this kind of advice, so I took a look at their backgrounds.

What I found was disappointing, but not surprising. Most authors and speakers have very little actual experience in depositions. I reached that conclusion by first searching the federal case management/electronic case filing database (CM/ECF) for cases in which they've appeared. The majority of them were identified as counsel in *fewer than fifty cases* in their entire career. Most were not involved in high-volume practices or in fields known for frequent trials. Some practice in areas where documents, not depositions, drive the outcome.

Don't believe me? Think of the most experienced litigator you can think of – someone you know, someone you've seen on TV – and search their name in the Advanced Party Search on PACER.gov. (That field retrieves lawyer appearances as well as actual party names.) Shocked by the result? Don't be. Most lawyers, even the most experienced litigators, just aren't hardcore front-line litigators.

Even in fairly large organizations with substantial numbers of trial lawyers, the skill associated with evaluating the need for, and method of conducting, depositions, is lacking. *E.g., Dalton v. Barrett,* 2019 WL 3069856, at *17 (W.D. Mo. July 12, 2019) (federal consent decree requiring training on depositions imposed where evidence showed no depositions were taken in 97% of criminal cases and lawyers lacked basic knowledge about when and how to take them).

My background is different. If you search the CM/ECF database in the two states where I practice, you'll find that I have appeared as chief counsel in more than a *thousand* federal cases. Over my career, my practice has been roughly divided equally between federal and state courts.

If I conservatively estimate, then, that I have appeared in as many state-court cases as I have in federal cases, you can safely conclude that I have appeared as chief counsel in more than two thousand cases. My practice area is high-volume and involves many depositions. The typical case I handle involves between 10 and 25 depositions. I estimate - based on the number of cases I have handled, and the average number of depositions in each - that I have probably taken or defended in excess of 20,000 depositions over my career. The basic math supports that. I originally chose the title for this series out of sheer modesty (and have kept the reference to 10,000 because the publisher does not want me to change the series title at this point).

My goal in drafting the practitioner's masterwork, *10,000 Depositions Later: The Premier Litigation Guide for Superior Deposition Practice*, was not to add another book to the shelf about the mechanics of taking depositions. Every other book does that. My goal was to discuss strategies and techniques you can't find elsewhere. Over the course of thousands and thousands of depositions, I've paid attention to what works and what doesn't and made many changes, sometimes almost imperceptible, in the way I approach the examination of witnesses. Over time I learned that some of those changes routinely led to big payoffs.

Some people say that if you focus on the basics, you'll do just fine. I think the opposite. If you're not looking for opportunities in the corners, where no one else is looking, if you're not looking for the micro-advantages that will make a difference in the close cases, and get you across the goal line, you're missing opportunities.

How big are small advantages? Consider this, from some Wall Street traders that recognize the value of searching out every conceivable advantage. A few years ago, a trading group spent almost half a billion dollars to pay for a relatively short underground cable that would transmit trades about *three milliseconds* faster than the cables currently in place.

Three milliseconds is three one-thousandths of a second.

This uptick in speed is so absurdly small as to be imperceptible. But the traders realized that, in a highly competitive field, every conceivable advantage that can be pursued must be pursued. They scrutinized every component of the trading process and had identified even minuscule changes that could make a difference. They overlooked nothing.

This systematic approach to successful investing is the difference between amateurs and pros. Small changes often result in the biggest gains. Professionals always look in the corners for micro-advantages. Professional athletes, once they establish their basic routines, immediately begin looking for ways to improve them.

They devote enormous resources to finding advantages. It may be a slight adjustment to the way they run, the way they throw, the way they hold the bat, hold the club or kick the ball. Once they make those changes, they begin looking for a way to make that change even better. It never stops. Professionals in every occupation know that continued success demands a constant hunt for improvements.

The practice of law is no different.

Princeton University Professor Daniel Kahneman, a Nobel Prize-winning psychologist and economist, contends that the only real way to develop true expertise is to (a) engage in regular practice, and (b) have swift feedback.

But the problem is that a litigator who takes a limited number of depositions each month, and who rarely tries cases, has neither. It is thus impossible for them to try a range of techniques in heavy practice and quickly see the results. My high-volume practice allows me to engage in frequent experimentation, to see over and over the results of my tactics. I see the results after the depositions, in settlement talks, in mediations, and in trial outcomes.

This advanced guide reveals what I know works in setting up and taking Rule 30(b)(6) depositions. You can use these expert-level techniques even if your deposition activity is limited. In other words, you can implement the most advanced deposition strategies in the profession without the need to devote thirty years in daily litigation warfare.

Try the techniques in this guide in your Rule 30(b)(6) depositions, and use them often, making your own adjustments to suit your style. If you are hesitant to implement them on a widespread basis, try them individually. You will see noticeable differences in the effectiveness of your examinations of organizational witnesses.

Some of these techniques will surely draw criticism or objection from opposing lawyers. Often the opposition will be the result of the lawyer's own inexperience. Opposing lawyers who've never encountered the tactics and strategies in this book likely suffer from myopic thinking, believing that if *they've never seen it, it must not be okay*.

But many of your adversaries have astonishingly limited experience, so what they've seen is no gauge of anything. Even lawyers in practice for a decade often lack appreciation for the most elemental notions of deposition practice. They think the rule of sequestration applies to depositions. (It does not.) They think you cannot independently audiotape depositions. (You can.) I could go on and on.

Use these Rule 30(b)(6) techniques aggressively. Stretch them even further than I have. Stand your ground. That's how you win.

Jim Garrity

THE FIVE-MINUTE GUIDE TO FRCP 30(B)(6) DEPOSITIONS

- §12.01 Overview and Purpose
- §12.02 Using Them To Assess Needs
- §12.03 One 30(b)(6) Depo? Or More?
- §12.04 Binding the Organization
- §12.05 Preparing the List of Topics
- §12.06 Basic Questions to Cover
- §12.07 Going Beyond the Topic List
- §12.08 Multiple 30(b)(6) Designees
- §12.09 Percipient Witnesses
- §12.10 30(b)(6) *Duces Tecum* Notices
- §12.11 Clarifying Audio, Video Use
- §12.12 Superior for Finding Evidence
- §12.13 30(b)(6) Witnesses at Trial
- §12.14 Sample Preparation Warning

- §12.15 30(b)(6) Deposition Defense
- §12.16 Burdensome Topic Lists
- §12.17 Taking Topic Lists Seriously
- §12.18 Lengthy Topic Lists
- §12.19 Topic-List Challenges
- §12.20 Duty to Prep Witnesses
- §12.21 Knowledge, Memory Failures
- §12.22 Using Privileged Documents
- §12.23 Choosing the Right Designee
- §12.24 Discovery in Lieu of 30(b)(6)
- §12.25 Designees as Fact Witnesses

- **§12.01 Overview and Purpose**

In this section, I talk about one of the most under-utilized tools in a litigator's arsenal: the designated-representative deposition.

This type of deposition is available when (a) your adversary is an organization and (b) you suspect individual fact witnesses will show up and claim they don't know or can't remember. Situations like that are the litigator's equivalent of "whack-a-mole," the child's game where hitting a toy mole that suddenly pops out of a hole on the board causes more to pop up elsewhere.

As an idiom, whack-a-mole refers to performing a repetitious and futile task, meaning that each time a specific job or task is completed, another one pops up. That's the concept when your corporate adversary has skillfully taught its witnesses to evade key questions.

Courts refer to this as "bandying" – essentially, the calculated plan of an adversary to have its individual witnesses each claim that someone else, not them, has the information needed.1 This is a frustrating experience, especially when you've burned through your available number of depositions and still don't have clear answers.[1]

The designated-representative deposition, colloquially referred to as a "30(b)(6)," is designed to help you avoid that experience. In the 30(b)(6) deposition:

- You prepare a notice listing the topics you want the entity to address
- •The entity must prepare and produce someone to fully testify about those topics
- •Answers are deemed answers of the organization itself
- •You generally get complete, detailed answers – rather than lots of "I don't knows" and "I don't remembers" - because severe penalties follow an organization's failure to properly prepare a designated representative.
- •Even if the entity produces multiple witnesses, which it can, to testify about your topics (because a single person may not be able to absorb enough information to do so), it still counts as a single

deposition. So rather than deposing ten witnesses – the default in federal court - you can conduct a single (30(b)(6) deposition and still have nine slots left.
- •You can in some jurisdictions take more than one 30(b)(6) deposition if needed.

If you regularly use this option, you know how useful it is. If you don't, your reaction might be, this is amazing. And that's the right reaction.

§12.02 Using Them To Assess Needs

The majority of my cases are in federal court, so I generally start with a 30(b)(6) deposition.

This way, I can quickly gather key information and use just one deposition slot to do so. The federal rules impose a default limit of ten depositions per party. That compels lawyers to carefully evaluate their choice of deponents.

If you face a cap on the number of depositions you can take, you should give serious thought to using a designated-representative deposition for your first slot, with a second and third round of individual fact-witness depositions. You'll want time after the 30(b)(6) to ponder the import of the testimony, and to determine whether you need additional interrogatories or document requests before you begin deposing fact witnesses.

Put another way, it may be unwise to schedule a 30(b)(6) at 9:00 AM on a given day and have fact witnesses lined up to start at 1:00 PM the same day. You will often learn a great deal in the 30(b)(6) that requires more paper discovery. That, in turn, may change your thinking about which witnesses should fill your remaining slots.

Further, scheduling a 30(b)(6) on a day by itself allows you the luxury of time to thoroughly explore every topic. You should not race through it. Your opponent's designated will have been prepared to answer detailed questions about each topic. It is essential to take the time you need to exhaust the entity's knowledge on them.

I also recommend, if you are permitted more than one 30(b)(6) deposition, that you set at least one more as your last deposition. This will allow you to wrap up any loose ends that remain.

§12.03 One 30(b)(6) Depo? Or More?

Note that some courts have held that you cannot take more than one 30(b)(6) deposition of the same entity. The reasoning is that, just as you cannot depose an individual more than once (without consent from the opposing party or court approval), you cannot repeatedly depose "the entity."

If your jurisdiction takes this position, you should make doubly sure that your 30(b)(6) notice lists all the topics you need the entity to address, and that you do not hold any back.[2]

I include the following lengthy quotation from a case holding that you are limited to one 30(b)(6) deposition per entity. My genuine apologies for the length, but the opinion contains the best complete analysis and reasoning for so limiting this type of deposition.

Thus it serves as both a warning that you may get only one and as a roadmap to the reasoning you'll need to argue around if you seek more. The discussion is from *State Farm Mut. Auto. Ins. Co. v. New Horizont, Inc.*, 254 F.R.D. 227, 234–36 (E.D. Pa. 2008) (and the "t" in "Horizont" is the correct spelling):

> A party need not normally obtain leave of court to take a deposition. Fed. R. Civ. P. 30(a)(1). The exceptions to this rule include the following:
>
> A party must obtain leave of court, and the court must grant leave to the extent consistent with Rule 26(b)(2):
>
> (A) if the parties have not stipulated to the deposition and:
>
> (i) the deposition would result in more than 10 depositions being taken under this rule ... by the plaintiffs, or by the defendants, or by the third-party defendants; [or] (ii) the deponent has already been deposed in the case; ... Fed. R. Civ. P. 30(a)(2).
>
> There is some disagreement as to whether the leave requirement in Rule 30(a)(2)(A)(ii) applies if a party seeks a second Rule 30(b)(6) deposition of a corporate party that

has already been deposed. The text of the rule and the advisory committee notes are silent on the relationship between Rule 30(a)(2)(A)(ii) and 30(b)(6). In contrast, regarding the immediately previous subsection allowing for a limit of 10 depositions without leave, the notes state: "A deposition under Rule 30(b)(6) should, for purposes of this limit, be treated as a single deposition even though more than one person may be designated to testify." Fed. R. Civ. P. 30(a)(2)(A) advisory committee's note (1993).

Reasoning from this note that "Rule 30(b)(6) depositions are different," at least one court has held that leave of court is not required when seeking a second Rule 30(b)(6) deposition of a corporate party who has already been deposed. See *Quality Aero Tech., Inc. v. Telemetrie Elektronik GmbH,* 212 F.R.D. 313, 319 (E.D.N.C. 2002); *see also Kimberly–Clark Corp. v. Tyco Healthcare Retail Group,* No. 05–985, 2007 WL 601837, at *3 n. 1 (granting leave but noting that "there is some question about whether leave of court is even required").

Other courts, however, have held to the contrary. See *Ameristar Jet Charter, Inc. v. Signal Composites, Inc.,* 244 F. 3d 189, 192 (1st Cir. 2001) (holding that it was not plainly wrong for the district court to quash a Rule 30(b)(6) subpoena when leave was not obtained); *In re Sulfuric Acid Antitrust Litig.,* No. 03–4576, 2005 WL 1994105, at *3–6 (N.D. Ill. Aug. 19, 2005) (following *Ameristar Jet,* rejecting *Quality Aero,* and citing

7 Moore's Federal Practice § 30.05(1)(c)). Among these courts is the only court in this circuit to address the issue. In *Sunny Isle Shopping Ctr., Inc. v. Xtra Super Food Cents. Inc.,* the Court noted in a footnote order that Rule 30(a)(2)(A)(ii) "has been held applicable to corporate depositions noticed pursuant to Rule 30(b)(6)." No. 98–154, 2002 WL 32349792, at *1 (D. Vi. July 24, 2002) (following *Ameristar Jet*).

The latter view appears to be the better one. Neither the text of the rule nor the committee's note exempts Rule 30(b)(6) depositions from the leave requirement in the event of a second deposition of a party already deposed. Rather, the notes state only that a Rule 30(b)(6) deposition should be treated as one deposition, no matter how many designees testify, for purposes of the 10-deposition limit. This limitation has a readily discernable logic, as large corporations with voluminous and complex documents may require testimony from multiple officers and custodians to provide comprehensive testimony regarding all matters "known or reasonably available to the organization." Fed. R. Civ. P. 30(b)(6). Thus, a contrary rule would place an unfair constraint on the number of depositions allowed to parties needing to conduct Rule 30(b)(6) depositions.

The same cannot be said for Rule 30(a)(2)(A)(ii). The policy against permitting a second deposition of an already-deposed deponent is equally applicable to depositions of individuals and organizations. Taking serial depositions of a single corporation may be as costly and burdensome, if not more so, as serial depositions of an individual. In both cases, each new deposition requires the deponent to spend time preparing for the deposition, traveling to the deposition, and providing testimony. In addition, allowing for serial depositions, whether of an individual or organization, provides the deposing party with an unfair strategic advantage, offering it multiple bites at the apple, each time with better information than the last. In short, the unfairness that manifests under Rule 30(a)(2)(A)(i), justifying an exception to the 10–deposition limit, does not manifest under Rule 30(a)(2)(A) (ii).

Here, Defendants have not sought leave of court to conduct an additional deposition of State Farm; thus the May 20, 2008 notice of deposition was improper. Plaintiffs' motion for protective order with respect to the May 20, 2008 notice could be granted on that basis. In the interest of efficiency, however, and in order to turn the litigation back to the merits, the Court will address the appropriateness of the discovery requested as if Defendants had sought leave of court.

B. *Rule 26(b)(2)(C)*

The Court may only grant leave to conduct multiple depositions of a single organization "to the extent consistent with Rule 26(b)(2)." *See* Fed. R. Civ. P. 30(a)(2).

Rule 26(b)(2) provides:

On motion or on its own, the court must limit the

frequency or extent of discovery otherwise allowed by these rules or by local rule if it determines that:

(i) the discovery sought is unreasonably cumulative or duplicative, or can be obtained from some other source that is more convenient, less burdensome, or less expensive;

(ii) the party seeking discovery has had ample opportunity to obtain the information by discovery in the action; or

(iii) the burden or expense of the proposed discovery outweighs its likely benefit, considering the needs of the case, the amount in controversy, the parties' resources, the importance of the issues at stake in the action, and the importance of the discovery in resolving the issues.

Fed. R. Civ. P. 26(b)(2)(C); *see also Melhorn v. N.J. Transit Rail Operations, Inc.,* 203 F.R.D. 176, 180 (E.D. Pa. 2001) ("Absent some showing of need or good reason for doing so, a deponent should not be required to appear for a second deposition.").

At the July 14, 2008 hearing, when asked why State Farm was not asked questions in connection with its non-fraud claims at the two prior Rule 30(b)(6) depositions, defense counsel responded as follows:

[T]his is a very complex matter. The way we decided to proceed is, *we decided to take the fraudulent issues which were related to the four counts of the complaint first, then see what happens* and then, you know, seek depositions on the other three counts of the complaints which are RICO conspiracy, unjust enrichment, and restitution which are side issues really. *We just simply decided to proceed in that manner.*

Hr'g Tr. 19:2–10, July 14, 2008.

The justification provided is insufficient. Defense counsel provides *no* reason, let alone a good reason, why the questions relating to State Farm's non-fraud claims were not noticed at the previous two Rule 30(b)(6) depositions; Defendants simply chose to proceed in such a manner. However, the Federal Rules do not contemplate the "wait-and-see" approach to discovery taken by Defendants. Such an idiosyncratic approach would permit Defendants, without having demonstrated any good cause for doing so, to avoid drafting a comprehensive notice of deposition and instead conduct depositions seriatim, thereby shifting costs to the opposing side, which would be forced to expend resources preparing for several Rule 30(b)(6) depositions, instead of one.

Therefore, the Court cannot grant Defendants leave to conduct additional Rule 30(b)(6) depositions of State Farm, as "the party seeking discovery has had ample opportunity to obtain the information by discovery in the action," and has not provided a good reason for failing to do so. Fed. R. Civ. P. 26(b)(2)(C). Accordingly, Plaintiffs' motion for protective order (doc. no. 381) has been granted.

There you have it - the argument for listing all your topics in a single notice. Again, be sure to check your jurisdiction.

You might be able to take more than one representative deposition. You might not.

Let's go over the basics for taking and defending this type of deposition.

§12.04 Binding the Organization

The basic purpose of a 30(b)(6) is to bind the organization and hold it accountable. The rule applies to any type of organization, including governmental entities. *FTC v. Vylah Tec LLC*, 2018 WL 7361111 (M.D. Fla. Dec. 18, 2018).

It differs from ordinary depositions of individuals because, in the typical deposition, you get little more than individual deponents' knowledge. Their testimony generally does not bind the organization. But an entity's 30(b)(6) designee *represents and is the voice of* the organization, just as individuals represent themselves. The designee ties down the entity's positions. Designees, then, will almost always testifying to matters beyond their personal experience.

§12.05 Preparing the List of Topics

The art in conducting this type of deposition is in the proper preparation of the topic list. The rule says you must describe the topics "with reasonable particularity." Courts say this means you must provide considerable detail and specificity.

Of course, the more specific you are, the more likely you end up with a long list of topics. It is a balance. As you gain experience drafting them, you will learn that a long, detailed list will draw complaints that your topics are excessive and burdensome. On the other hand, a shorter, broad-brush list will draw objections that your list is too vague and that the entity does not know how to prepare its designee.

I say again, it's a balance.

How many topics are too many? It depends on the type of case, the complexity of the issues, the number of parties, and other factors. There is no set limit. If you draw objections for one reason or the other, your judge will take a practical approach, balancing your interest in complete answers, the organization's burden in providing them, and the answers actually given. Be mindful, too, that there is discussion under way of amending Rule 30(b)(6) to require the parties to confer about the number of topics, the description of the topics, and the identity of the witnesses to be produced. This is a topic of hot debate, and it is not clear the amendment will be approved. But it's useful to know about it.[2]

But a long list of topics isn't automatically an inappropriate one. Sometimes, there are just many topics to cover.

To illustrate, Facebook and a virtual reality company – codefendants in a lawsuit - served 30(b)(6) notices to the plaintiff that contained 86 topics apiece, for a total of 172 topics.

The court said the number wasn't unreasonable given that the operative complaint was approximately 200 paragraphs, with multiple claims against multiple parties. *Zenimax Media, Inc. v. Oculus VR LLC*, 2016 WL 11476858 (N.D. Texas Jan.

27, 2017). It also approved the use of 30(b)(6) topics as legal contention inquiries (e.g., "Tell us any and all facts supporting your claims"), which is noteworthy because most courts do not allow legal contention questions in depositions.

And in another case, the judge seemed unperturbed by a topic list with 52 topics, but did require the plaintiff to revise the list. The examples in the opinion are instructive. *Klopman-Baerselman v. Air & Liquid Systems Corp.*, 2019 WL 3717902 (W. D. Wash. 2019).

The bottom line? Drafting topic lists is a skill that grows with practice. You should strive to achieve balance in the length and complexity of your topics, so the responding entity can reasonably prepare its witnesses. The ideal list is specific enough to result in useful information, and general enough to allow you to drill down into the topics without triggering incessant objections that your questions are beyond the scope of the topic.

§12.06 Basic Questions to Cover

The substantive questions you ask the designee will depend on your case. But there are general background questions to ask all designees, about both their background and their relationship to the organization.

It's also important to confirm their understanding that they are the voice of the organization. You will occasionally encounter a designee with a deer-in-the-headlights look, as if to say they have no idea what you are talking about. That is never a good sign, but it's important to have that conversation to create a record if the witness was not properly prepared

Sample preliminary lines of inquiry include the following:

•Job history with, and relationship to, the entity; all positions held, pending or anticipated pay increases or position changes; disciplinary history

•Confirmation that witnesses understand they speak for organization; confirmation regarding topics that witness is/is not prepared to testify about

Next, before delving into the substantive designated topics, you should inquire about witness preparation efforts. Some suggested questions and topics for this segment:

•What did you do to prepare?

•Did you meet with anyone to prepare for your testimony?

•Identify each person by name and job title (including counsel)

•Dates of, and length of, each such meeting

•Documents reviewed and notes taken by anyone

•Identities of anyone else in the room or on the phone

•Contacts with former employees, third parties to prepare

•Notes taken at any point since designation; where and when

•Documents reviewed or provided

•Clarify which were provided and which were obtained or located by the deponent

•Did witness help respond to discovery generally in the case

•Review pleadings, discovery, deposition transcripts?

- Documents the witness reviewed.
- Documents supporting the witness' testimony; what they are and where they are located

§12.07 Going Beyond the Topic List

Can you ask the designee questions that go beyond the topics you attached to the notice? Most courts say yes.

If your questions go beyond the list, then general deposition rules apply and the witness is no longer speaking for the entity. I recommend that when preparing your notice, you further state (as I do) that in addition to the listed topics, the representatives produced will be asked other questions outside the scope of the notice and based on their own personal knowledge. That will avoid unfounded arguments during the deposition about whether you can properly exceed the designated list of topics.

But if you do, I strongly recommend that you do so after finishing your questions to the designers-as-designee. Once you're done asking the witness to speak as the organization then announce or otherwise note for the record that you are now asking the witness questions from the witness' own personal knowledge. Why? To avoid confusion about which questions were answered as the entity and which were answered by the witness personally.

Here's an excellent overview of the issue from a Florida federal court in 2018, in the case *Fed. Trade Comm'n v. Vylah*

Tec LLC, No. 2017-cv-228-FT-MPA-MRM, 2018 WL 7361111, at *5 (M.D. Fla. Dec. 18, 2018):

> Rule 30(b)(6) does not limit what can be asked at a deposition. *McMahon v. Presidential Airways, Inc.*, No. 6:05-cv-1002-Orl-28JGC, 2006 WL 5359797, at *4 (M.D. Fla. Jan. 18, 2006) ("The requirement that the party noticing the deposition 'describe with reasonable particularity the matters on which the examination is requested' does not limit the scope of the deposition to the contents of the notice."); *see also Bank of Am., N.A. v. Russo*, No. 6:11-cv-734-Orl-22GJK, 2013 WL 12158131, at *7 (M.D. Fla. Apr. 2, 2013); *King*, 161 F.R.D. at 476.
>
> Rather, Rule 30(b)(6) simply defines a corporation's "duty to produce a representative who can answer questions that are both within the scope of the matters described in the notice and are 'known or reasonably available' to the corporation." *King*, 161 F.R.D. at 476.
>
> Thus, "[i]f the examining party asks questions outside the scope of the matters described in the notice, the general deposition rules govern (*i.e.*, Fed. R. Civ. P. 26(b)(1)), so that relevant questions may be asked and no special protection is conferred on a deponent by virtue of the fact that the deposition was noticed under 30(b)(6)." *Id.* "[I]f the deponent does not know the answer to questions outside the scope of the matters described in the notice, then that is the examining party's problem." *Id.*

The Court finds that Plaintiff's counsel's instructions to Mr. Adler not to answer questions that fell outside the scope of the noticed deposition topics in his representative capacity were improper. (*See, e.g.*, 228:21-229:20; 235:1-236:3). The fact that Mr. Adler was permitted to answer the questions in his "personal" or "individual" capacity does not cure or ameliorate this impropriety. A Rule 30(b)(6) witness represents the collective knowledge of the entity and provides testimony that is binding on the *entity*, not the individual. *See QBE Ins. Corp.*, 277 F.R.D. at 688; *Continental Cas. Co. v. First Fin. Emp. Leasing, Inc.*, 716 F. Supp. 2d 1176, 1189 (M.D. Fla. 2010).

The Court finds that in the context of this deposition, the instruction not to answer questions in a representative capacity was improper because the witness clearly had information responsive to the questions posed – as evinced by the fact that he answered them – and Plaintiff offers no explanation for why that factual information could not have been offered through the same witness in a representative capacity in the context of this particular Rule 30(b)(6) deposition.

In other words, if the witness knows the information in his individual capacity, then the entity also has that same information and should be able to offer it through the same witness testifying in a representative capacity even if the information falls outside one of the duly noticed deposition topics.

As noted above, no special protection is conferred on a deponent by virtue of the fact that the deposition was noticed under 30(b)(6). It would certainly be different if the witness sitting in a representative capacity was unable to answer the question fully or *at all* because the information sought fell outside the noticed deposition topics and the witness was not otherwise prepared or sufficiently knowledgeable to provide an answer on behalf of the entity.

But here, the questions were relevant, and the witness actually had answers. Accordingly, the Court finds that the instruction not to answer in a representative capacity was improper.

§12.08 Multiple 30(b)(6) Designees

The responding entity must designate a representative or representatives to address the topics. It is up to the organization, not you, to choose the representatives and decide whether one or more are needed to fully address the inquiries.

The designee(s) produced do not need personal knowledge about the topics. Remember they are speaking for the organization, not themselves. So lawyers must often sit down with the people chosen by the entity and ensure they've been spoon-fed enough information to answer your questions.

An organization cannot refuse to comply with your notice by asserting that there is no one that has the information you need. And if it appears they must prepare more than one person, they are obligated to do so. *Catalina Rental Apartments, Inc. v. Pac. Ins. Co.*, No. 06-20532 CIV, 2007 WL 917272, at *2 (S.D. Fla. Mar. 23, 2007) ("If it becomes obvious that one corporate designee is deficient, the corporation is obligated to provide a substitute or additional designees to comply with the corporation's obligations under Rule 30(b)(6).").

If the entity refuses to designate a witness or witnesses, the remedy is to seek an order compelling designation. *See Ortiz v. Cybex International, Inc., 2018 WL 2448130 (D. Puerto Rico May 30, 2018).*

§12.09 Percipient Witnesses

When your case revolves around events personally witnessed by individuals - such as an accident, fight, conversation or similar event - your interests are usually better served by deposing the eyewitness(es), rather than pursuing the information from a corporate designee. In legal parlance, eyewitnesses are referred to as "percipient witnesses" - those who personally perceived the events.

The question to ask in deciding whether to use FRCP 30(b)(6), or to just set individual depositions is this: Would a 30(b)(6) deponent be forced to interview eyewitnesses in detail and then simply recount (second-hand) the individualized observations of multiple people? Or is the topic one for which there is an institutional answer or position that could be better gathered by the organization and easily presented through a single witness, much like an interrogatory answer?

Where you can depose actual eyewitnesses, and where they may have differing individual perspectives, a judge upon receipt of a motion for protective order may prevent you from setting a 30(b)(6), if doing so would force the entity to conduct interviews and develop a singular account.

This issue was discussed in excellent detail in *Jones v. US Border Patrol Agent Gerardo Hernandez*, Case 3:16-CV-01986-W-WVG, Order On Discovery Dispute FRCP 30(b)(6) Deposition Notice (CM/ECF Doc. 84) (S.D. Ca., order filed Jan 23. 2018). This order is well worth reading if you face this issue.

§12.10 30(b)(6) Duces Tecum Notices

Can you require designee witnesses to bring documents with them? Yes.

Just as with any other deposition, you can require designees to produce documents by noticing the deposition *duces tecum. Richardson v. Rock City Mech. Co., LLC*, No. CV 3-09-0092, 2010 WL 711830, at *4 (M.D. Tenn. Feb. 24, 2010) ("There is no reason to believe that a Rule 30(b)(6) deposition is not subject to Rule 30(b)(2).")

Just attach a list of the documents to the notice. What might you ask the designee to bring? Many lawyers require the production of all documents the designee used to prepare for the deposition, *e.g.,* "All documents the designee was provided or used to prepare to testify about topics 1 - 25."

When serving this on a party, you are effectively grafting a Rule 34 request for production of documents onto your deposition notice. Be mindful that, unless you have agreement otherwise, you must allow the full period for response to a request for production if you want the party designee to bring documents. In other words, you cannot short-circuit the time the opposing party would have to respond for a request for production by making the request within a 30(b)(6) notice.3

§12.11 Clarifying Audio, Video Use

If you plan to record the deposition using audio or video devices, be sure your deposition notice clearly says so. Your notice should also clearly say that it will be used for all permissible purposes, including discovery and trial.

§12.12 Superior for Finding Evidence

A 30(b)(6) deposition can be of great value in determining how an organization stores and retrieves information. It is particularly useful now that so much evidence is stored digitally. Thus one of your standard topics should be the manner in which information is stored, retrieved, archived and deleted on the entity's computer systems. In fact, you may not get straight answers to these questions unless you schedule a representative deposition.

To get you started, here is some sample language you might use in your notice on the topic of information storage and retrieval. You are welcome to use this language verbatim:

Corporate representative, designated under Rule 30(b)(6) as knowledgeable about how [Entity] stores information on mail systems, archives, local drives, shared networks, portable devices, removable media and databases. Many devices require different search terms because they store and retrieve information differently and often use or require different search term characteristics (e.g., Boolean constructs, proximity searches, "stemming," and fielded searches, to name a few that come to mind. Each device and system may require different approaches to ensure all data is retrieved properly. Plaintiff will also examine the witness about the software programs used in the relevant store by managers and supervisors in the store(s) where Plaintiff worked; how emails, memos, records and reports are stored, backed up and retrieved, including the format for storage and the methods including search terms for retrieval. Plaintiff will examine the witness about similar topics for market managers and HR personnel. Plaintiff will examine the witness about the witness' background, education and experience; position(s) held within [Entity]; how long information is stored, specific to emails, memos, counseling and coaching memos and evaluations; how coachings, counselings, suspensions, firings and similar adverse employment action is maintained and searched on [Entity] systems, including the steps needed to conduct specific searches, such as for all persons under a particular manager or in a particular store who have been disciplined, coached, suspended, been given decision days or fired for the same or similar offenses; how many times, and for what, a manager has imposed discipline, coachings or counselings, and related inquiries.

Adjust as you see fit to meet your circumstances.

§12.13 30(b)(6) Witnesses at Trial

Can you call the corporate designee who appeared for your 30(b)(6) deposition as a witness at trial - to speak for the company as they did in deposition? Courts vary, but the broad consensus seems to be yes.

Considering that the deponent comes speaking for the entity, and that there is no distinction between the representative and the company, the testimony on behalf of the entity is a statement of a party opponent and not hearsay when offered by the adversary. *See Ortiz v. Cybex International, Inc., 2018 WL 2448130 (D. Puerto Rico May 30, 2018). citing Sprint Comm v. Theglobe.com, Inc 236 FRD 524.*

Be mindful of the possibility that your adversary may also attempt to call its 30(b)(6) witnesses at trial. On this note, *see* Rule 32(a)(2), and check out another excellent resource, *Is Live Trial Testimony Permissible? A Primer on 30(b)(6) Witnesses*, by Lauren Bragin, DRI for the Defense, 57 No. 4, DRI For Def. 26 (April 2015).

§12.14 Sample Preparation Warning

You will occasionally encounter some lawyers who have not been on the receiving end of a 30(b)(6) deposition request. They will not appreciate the preparation required in producing a designee. So, depending on whether tactical considerations are best served by a fully-loaded designee or one shooting blanks, you may wish to add the following cautionary language at the back of the notice:

Notice Regarding Preparation of Fed. R. Civ. P. 30(b)(6) Designees

In response to this deposition notice pursuant to Rule 30(b)(6), which reasonably particularizes the subjects of the intended inquiry, the responding party has a duty "to make a conscientious, good-faith effort to designate knowledgeable persons for Rule 30(b)(6) depositions and to prepare them to fully and unevasively answer questions about the designated subject matter." *Starlight Int'l Inc. v. Herlihy*, 186 F.R.D. 626, 639 (D. Kan. 1999). "Not only must the organization designate a witness, but it is responsible also to prepare the witness to answer questions on the topics identified and present the organization's knowledge on those topics." Wright, Miller & Marcus, 8A FED. PRACTICE & PROCEDURE CIV. 2d § 2103. The 30(b)(6) deponent must not only testify about facts within the organization's knowledge, "but also its subjective beliefs and opinions…[to] provide its interpretation of documents and events." *United States v. Taylor*, 166 F.R.D. 365, 361 (M.D.N.C. 1996).

Under, Rule 30(b)(6) [I]f the persons designated by the corporation do not possess personal knowledge of the matters set out in the deposition notice, the corporation is obligated to prepare the designees so that they may give knowledgeable and binding answers for the corporation. Thus, the duty to present and prepare a Rule 30(b)(6) designee goes beyond matters personally known to that designee or to matters in which that designee was personally involved. *DHL Express (USA), Inc. v. Express Save Industries Inc.*, 2009 U.S. Dist. LEXIS 102981, 2009 WL 3418148 (S.D. Fla. Oct. 19, 2009) (internal quotations and citations omitted). *EEOC v. Winn-Dixie, Inc.*, 2010 U.S. Dist. LEXIS 53005 (S.D. Ala. May 28, 2010).

"The party responding to a 30(b)(6) deposition notice 'must prepare deponents by having them review prior fact witness deposition testimony as well as documents and depositions, exhibits.'" *Calzaturficio S.C.A.R.P.A. S.P.A. v. Fabiano Shoe Co.*, 201 F.R.D. 33, 37 (D. Mass. 2001), quoting *Prokosch v. Catalina Lighting, Inc.*, 193 F.R.D. 633, 639 (D. Minn. 2000), quoted in *Chick-Fil-A v. ExxonMobil Corp.*, 2009 U.S. Dist. LEXIS 109588 (S.D. Fla. Nov. 10, 2009). "The burden upon the responding party, to prepare a knowledgeable Rule 30(b)(6) witness, may be an onerous one, but we are not aware of any less onerous means of assuring that the position of a corporation that is involved in litigation, can be fully and fairly explored." Id. at 638. The corporation and its counsel have a duty to prepare the witness so that he or she is able to give "complete, knowledgeable and binding answers on behalf of the corporation." *Continental Cas. Co. v. Compass Bank*, 2006 U.S. Dist. LEXIS 12288, 2006 WL 533510 * 18 (S.D.

Ala. March 3, 2006) citing, *Marker v. Union Fidelity Life Ins. Co.*, 125 F.R.D. 121, 126 (M.D.N.C. 1989). The person being deposed is required to testify about the knowledge of the corporation as an entity and not his or her own knowledge. Id. An individual identified as a Rule 30(b)(6) witness may be called on to answer questions known to the corporation but not to himself personally. The duty to prepare the Rule 30(b)(6) witness properly attaches to the deponent corporation. Calzaturficio, Inc., 201 F.R.D. at 37.

"Producing an unprepared witness is tantamount to a failure to appear at a deposition." *Starlight Int'l Inc. v. Herlihy*, 186 F.R.D. 626, 639 (D. Kan. 1999). In response to Rule 30(b)(6) deposition notices, parties are required "to have persons testify on its behalf as to all matters known or reasonably available to it and, therefore implicitly require such persons to review all matters known or reasonably available to it in preparation for the Rule 30 (b)(6) deposition." Taylor, 166 F.R.D. at 362.

The 30(b)(6) deposition requires a party to present a properly prepared witness whose testimony is binding on the corporation. E.g., *Calzaturficio*, 201 F.R.D. at 37. The organization has an affirmative duty to prepare the designated deponents so they can give full, complete, and non-evasive answers to questions posed regarding the relevant subject matter. 7 MOORE'S FEDERAL PRACTICE, § 30.25[3] at 30.68 (emphasis added) [hereinafter "Moore's"]. See, *Prokosch v. Catalina Lighting, Inc.*, 193 F.R.D. 633, 638 (D. Minn. 2000). A party is free to designate anyone who consents to testify on its behalf, so long as the designated witness is prepared to testify on behalf of that party as to the matters upon which examination is requested in the notice.

The duties imposed by Rule 30(b)(6), therefore, are: (1) the deponent must be knowledgeable on the subject matter identified as the area of inquiry; (2) the designating party must designate more than one deponent if necessary in order to respond to the relevant areas of inquiry specified by the party requesting the deposition; (3) the designating party must prepare the witness to testify on matters not only known by the deponent, but those that should be known by the designating party; and (4) the designating party must substitute an appropriate deponent when it becomes apparent that the previous deponent is unable to respond to certain relevant areas of inquiry. Id. § 30.25[3] at 30-68 (emphasis added).

§12.15 30(b)(6) Deposition Defense

Now let's take a look at this kind of deposition from the perspective of the lawyer defending it. There are several considerations in responding to the list of topics, in choosing those who will appear, and in preparing them.

§12.16 Burdensome Topic Lists

The chief problem you will encounter in defending designee depositions arises because many litigators are not accustomed to crafting 30(b)(6) topic lists. This will be immediately obvious.

In fact, the first several tries by an attorney to draft a topic list usually results in a list that seems to cover every claim, defense, and fact in the entire case.

You may also see language like "including but not limited to...." This is generally improper because you have no way to determine the outer limits of the examination. Deficient topic lists also often lack geographic and temporal limits.

Nonetheless, you must take the list of topics seriously because you are obligated to produce witnesses who can speak to them unless you negotiate something better with the opposing lawyer or seek court intervention.

§12.17 Taking Topic Lists Seriously

Remember that the testimony of your designees are the official, binding answers of the organization. And as I pointed out elsewhere in this book, answers of "I don't know" and "I don't remember" can bind your client and bar it from presenting substantive testimony on the topics to which your designee claims a lack of knowledge or recollection. Organizations are bound by their 30(b)(6) testimony. Just as individual witnesses cannot come into a courtroom with a suddenly-improved memory, nor can the entity. Some courts have held that if your designated representative cannot answer questions in the deposition, the entity cannot present witnesses to provide that information at trial. You could be stuck with the memory failures. At best, such answers could result in uncomfortable impeachment of your witnesses.

§12.18 Lengthy Topic Lists

Avoid undue fixation on the number of topics. Courts have approved deposition notices for dozens of topics. *E.g., Tamburri v. SunTrust Mortg. Inc.*, No. C-11-02899 JST DMR, 2013 WL 1616106, at *2 (N.D. Cal. Apr. 15, 2013) (approving fifty topics); *Krasney v. Nationwide Mut. Ins. Co.,* No. 3:06 CV 1164 JBA, 2007 WL 4365677, at *1 (D. Conn. Dec. 11, 2007) (approving 40 topics).

Focus instead on the topics phrasings, and look for deficiencies. Inappropriate phrases, and other flaws to look out for, include:
- "All defenses"
- "All claims"
- "Any and all"
- "Including but not limited to"
- "All allegations in the Complaint"
- "All facts supporting your claims/defenses"
- All denials and Affirmative Defendants
- The absence of a specific date range
- The absence of geographic limitations

- The absence of a limit to the department, office or other compartment at issue
- Language calling for privileged information

In essence, you are using the same analysis you would for an ordinary request for production of documents or set of interrogatories. The list of topics in a 30(b)(6) deposition is subject to the same general objections you make in response to any discovery request. But just as judges vary in ruling on discovery requests, they may also vary in deeming specific topics proper or not. However the topics are words, the key is deciding whether as written they are inappropriate.4

§12.19 Topic-List Challenges

What is the proper procedure for opposing an objectionable 30(b)(6) topic list? Serve objections? Or seek a protective order? Courts differ, but the majority say you must seek a protective order.

Representative of courts that say merely serving objections is sufficient is the decision in *Kaplan v. Nautilus Insurance Company*, No. 17-CV-24453, 2018 WL 6445886, at *1 (S.D. Fla. Sept. 17, 2018), where the court said, "When a party objects to the scope of a 30(b)(6) deposition notice, courts have found that the proper means for raising the dispute is by timely serving those objections upon the opposing party in advance of the deposition, not by filing a motion for protective order seeking anticipatory review before the deposition."

Many courts are critical of this approach because it allows

lawyers to serve objections at the last minute and thwart the effectiveness of 30(b)(6) depositions. Such courts say that if you are going to challenge the list, you must seek court intervention, and risk being sanctioned for doing so. The obligation to involve the court serves as a deterrent to obstructive objection tactics.

A federal judge in his 2018 Order Regarding Discovery Dispute on Plaintiff's Proposed Rule 30(b)(6) Deposition Topics said the recipient of an offending 30(b)(6) notice *must* seek a protective order before the scheduled deposition. *See Rutherford, et al v. Evans Hotels LLC, et al*, No. 18CV435-JLS(MSB), 2018 WL 6246516 at *3 (S.D. Cal. Nov. 29, 2018).

For other cases following this rule, see *Robinson v. Quicken Loans, Inc.*, No. 3:12–cv–00981, 2013 WL 1776100, at *3 (S.D. W. Va. Apr. 25, 2013); *New England Carpenters Health Benefits Fund v. First DataBank, Inc.*, 242 F.R.D. 164, 166 (D. Mass. 2007).). ("Put simply and clearly, absent agreement, a party who for one reason or another does not wish to comply with a notice of deposition must seek a protective order.")

These courts have held it insufficient to serve objections and then declare that a witness will only testify within the scope of its objections. One court said such objections ". . exhibit exactly the type of technical objection-crafting the Rules seek to deter and for which Rule 37 sanctions were created." *Beach Mart, Inc. v. L & L Wings, Inc.*, 302 F.R.D. 396,

406–07 (E.D.N.C. 2014) Another court similarly held objections improper. *Espy v. Mformation Techs., Inc.*, No. 08-2211-EFM-DWB, 2010 WL 1488555, at *3 (D. Kan. Apr. 13, 2010)

So which path to take? It depends on your particular jurisdiction. If I were in a jurisdiction where the law was not yet settled, I might do both - file a motion for a protective order, candidly admitting my uncertainty about which line of cases will be followed, and at the same time, file and serve written objections.

Corporate representative depositions can make or break a case because the witness is the voice of the entity. So I would not hesitate to take both paths at the same time to ensure that I did not leave my client unprotected by choosing one or the other.

§12.20 Duty to Prep Witnesses

While the rule may not require the designers to answer every conceivable question - it speaks of the obligation to attest to matters known or "reasonably available to the organization" - it does require a concerted good-faith effort on your part to collect information by reviewing documents and interviewing employees with personal knowledge, just as an entity does in answering interrogatories.

This will often require a lengthy and time-consuming effort on your part to choose and prepare the designee(s). You are free to designate current or former employees. But whoever your designate, your obligation is to ensure they can answer the topics thoroughly.

Basic preparation includes the following:
1. Explaining the deposition process thoroughly
2. Explaining the role of 30(b)(6) witnesses
3. Carefully reviewing the topic list
4. Conducting a mock deposition
5. Determining the extent of elaboration on answers
6. Addressing expressions of opinion or belief
7. Addressing the entity's stance on issues
8. Covering topics related to but beyond the topic list, as some courts consider the list to be the bare minimum that could be explored. *ChrMar Sys. Inc v. Cisco Sys, Inc.* 312 F.R.D. 560 (N.D. Cal. 2016) and *Fed. Deposit Ins. Corp. v. Giancola* 2015 WL 5559804 (N.D. Ill. Sep. 18, 2016)

§12.21 Knowledge, Memory Failures

There may be occasions where your designee says the entity lacks knowledge of a certain fact. It may simply not know, or it may simply have no answer. *Catalina Rental Apartments, Inc. v. Pac. Ins. Co.*, No. 06-20532 CIV, 2007 WL 917272, at *2 (S.D. Fla. Mar. 23, 2007). But where this occurs, the adversary may be allowed to point to that inability to answer on summary judgment and at trial.

The adversary may also seek an order *in limine* flatly barring the entity from presenting evidence at trial on the topics it could not answer in the 30(b)(6) deposition. *See*

Kartagener v. Carnival Corporation, 380 F. Supp. 3d 1290 (S. D. Fla. 2019) *(d*efendant precluded from taking position at trial—including introduction of testimony and exhibits—on 30(b)(6) topics which witnesses could not address; entity's inability to speak to topics in deposition will equally silence it at trial).

§12.22 Using Privileged Documents

You may wish to exercise caution in preparing the witness or witnesses with privileged documents. Otherwise, the privilege may be waived as to those documents.

On the other hand, it is no answer to a 30(b)(6) deposition notice to claim that relevant documents or investigations are privileged and that therefore no knowledgeable witness can be produced. Similarly, the mere fact that you might prepare a witness or witnesses for a 30(b)(6) deposition would not create an attorney-client privilege as to the facts of the case that the attorney and the witness might discuss.

§12.23 Choosing the Right Designee

Where possible, my preference is to designate a single witness. This avoids the risks of confusion or conflicts where multiple designees are selected. It can also save you the possible nightmare of multiple seven-hour depositions under the federal rules, to the extent your jurisdiction considers each appearance by a separate designee as a new deposition.

My ideal designated representatives have certain testimony-friendly qualities. They:

1. are experienced litigation witnesses
2. are not easily flustered
3. have excellent memories
4. speak with clarity and precision
5. are patient
6. can tolerate lengthy or aggressive examinations

I avoid designees who are involved in legal strategy for the organization. While such individuals are otherwise perfect because they meet my basic criteria, they might also give testimony that could result in the inadvertent waiver of work-product or attorney-client privilege. This is because they might have problems mixing personal and corporate knowledge in this respect. That could allow the opposing lawyer to stray far beyond the listed topics.

§12.24 Discovery in Lieu of 30(b)(6)

What if, after reviewing the list of topics, you conclude that other fact witnesses for the organization have already testified about those areas? Can you simply designate that deposition testimony in place of preparing and producing a live witness? I am not aware of the case that says this is inappropriate as a bright-line matter, but I would never recommend it.

First, fact witnesses do not speak for the entity. Second, an ordinary fact witness is not required to review all pertinent documents before appearing. A designated representative is.

Third, it is unlikely that ordinary depositions of fact witnesses resulted in answers that are as thorough and complete as if the witness had been deposed under Rule 30(b)(6). Fourth, even if you have previously served interrogatory answers and documents on the same topics as the 30(b)(6) notice, you must still prepare and produce a representative if the adversary insists. *E.g., CRST Expedited, Inc. v. Swift Transportation Co. of Arizona, LLC*, No. 17-CV-25-CJW-KEM, 2019 WL 2714508, at *5 (N.D. Iowa Mar. 6, 2019) (producing documents and responding to written discovery is not a substitute for providing a thoroughly educated Rule 30(b)(6) deponent).

So, you risk sanctions if you represent an entity and fail to produce a properly-prepared representative witness. Remember that courts have said that the failure to present a properly-prepared witness is equivalent to failing to present any witness whatsoever at the deposition. Under Rule 37(d), your opponent can seek sanctions without first filing a motion to compel a better deposition. *E.g., Scott v Wabash National Corporation*, 2007 WL 9773389; *In re Brican Am. LLC Equip. Leave Litig.*, 2013 WL 5519980 (S.D. Fla. Oct. 1, 2013) (sanctions imposed against entity for merely designating prior fact witness depositions instead of presenting properly-informed representative for 30(b)(6) deposition); *see also Sciarretta v. Lincoln Nat. Life Ins. Co.*, 778 F. 3d 1205, 1211 (11th Cir. 2015) (affirming $850,000 in sanctions against party relating to failure to properly prepare designated representative under Rule 30(b)(6)).

§12.25 Designees as Fact Witnesses

In some cases, your adversary may attempt to re-depose - as a fact witness - the same person you designated as your 30(b)(6) representative. Is this permissible? Should you object?

The clear answer is maybe. The question is whether the representative has substantial additional personal knowledge. Otherwise, a second deposition makes little sense.

This issue arose in *R.D. v. Shohola Camp Ground and Resort*, Case No. 3:16-CV-1056, 2017 WL 1550034 (M.D. Pa. May 1, 2017). There the plaintiff wanted to depose the witness, a records custodian, first under Fed. R. Civ. P. 30(b)(6) about corporate records and, separately, a second time as a fact witness. The defendant argued the witness should be forced to sit for deposition just once.

Note, as we progress here, that this plaintiff signaled in advance his intention to depose the representative on an individual basis later. So the question of "one, or two?" arose before either deposition began, and was thus a hypothetical one at that point for the court.

The judge took the middle ground, ruling that he would only allow one deposition initially. But he permitted the plaintiff to seek a second deposition if there was a legitimate basis. The judge pointed out that discovery rulings were within his sound discretion, and it was not clear whether the deponent had sufficient personal knowledge to justify a second deposition.

In that case, combining the two kinds of depositions made

sense because the 30(b)(6) piece was limited to some brief questions about records.

But conducting a combined 30(b)(6) and fact deposition of a single deponent poses risks to both plaintiff and defendant. For the defense, it leaves open the possibility that loose comments by the witness are deemed testimony of the company. For the plaintiff, it can make separating statements that bind the company and those that made individually a messy job. Plaintiffs need clean facts and testimony. Defendants need bright-line protection against liability. Combining corporate representative and fact witness depositions is risky business across the board.

~

---

1. A useful case on the topic of bandying is *Updike v. Clackamas County*, No. 3:15-CV-723-SI, 2016 U.S. Dist. LEXIS 2783 at *4-5 (D. Or. Jan 11. 2016). You can find the specific Opinion and Order on PACER at Document 40.
2. The proposed amendments were published in August 2018 by the federal Committee on Rules of Practice and Procedure of the Judicial Conference of the United States. According to the Committee's August 15, 2018 Memorandum requesting public comment on the proposed change, "If approved, with or without revision, by the relevant advisory committee, the Committee on Rules of Practice and Procedure, the Judicial Conference, and the Supreme Court, the proposed amendments would become effective on December 1, 2020, if Congress does not act to defer, modify, or reject them."

   The proposed amendment would add the following language (with the new language in italics): "B*efore or promptly after the notice or subpoena is served, and continuing as necessary,* the serving party and *the organization must confer in good faith about the number and description of the matters for examination and the identity of each person the organization will designate to testify.* A subpoena must advise a nonparty organization of its duty to make this designation *and to confer with the serving party."*

AFTERWORD

We hope you found this Five-Minute Guide useful. It's one of a series of short, expert-level guides authored by Jim Garrity, the nation's leading expert on deposition science and practice.

The Five-Minute Guides fill a critical gap for litigators. Many of you told us you wanted something thorough and current but also short and to the point. You also told us you wanted something you can easily slip into your bag and take with you to depositions.

We heard you. The Five-Minute Guide series is the result, and we are genuinely grateful to you for purchasing it. (Don't forget that you can also buy his complete 490-page practitioner's guide on expert-level deposition strategies and tactics on Amazon. Search for *10,000 Depositions Later: The Premier Litigation Guide for Superior Deposition Practice.*)

A few final thoughts.

Jim Garrity invites input. If you have tactics or strategies that you find effective in taking or defending depositions, Jim would love to hear about them, and possibly include them in the next revision of this book. You can communicate with him directly at Jim@JimGarrityLaw.com. (And if you have questions about specific deposition problems you're encountering, email him about those as well. He often responds directly, and may (with your prior express approval) post a generalized, non-identifiable response on the book's Facebook page to alert others to the problems and to his solutions.

Like and follow the Facebook page. Be sure to stop by the free companion Facebook page to this book. That's where Garrity regularly posts new tactics, strategies, and cases on depositions. Like and follow at www.Facebook/TenThousandDepositionsBook to receive his posts in your news feed.

Let us add you to our limited mailing list. A few times each year, Jim Garrity sends updates about new strategies and cases to a free, subscription-email group of litigators who've signed up to receive them. These come out before they appear on the Facebook page or in the next edition of the book. We'd love to add you to the list. He sends no more than four per year, and, typically, it's half that because he respects your time. Please email Josh Siskind, Director of Marketing, at JoshSiskind@RossAndRubin.com with "Please add me to the private email group mailing list" in the subject line. That's it. It's completely free.

Ask for a seminar. Jim Garrity regularly conducts live,

full-day deposition seminars around the country. These programs receive rave reviews because they allow for direct interaction between Jim and litigators interested in sharpening their deposition skills. They also feature discussions of his newest insights and of cases released since the publication of this book. Interested? Reach out to Josh Siskind, our marketing director, at JoshSiskind@RossAndRubin.com for details.

Thank you again.

Ross and Rubin Publishers, LLC

Made in the USA
Monee, IL
06 December 2024